Contents

Any words appearing in the text in bold,
like this, are explained in the Glossary.
You can also look out for them in the 'In the
know' box at the bottom of each page.

All sorts of drugs

What do you think?

Drugs are all around us and are used for all sorts of reasons. Some drugs are good for you and can be good for your health if taken in the correct way. Other drugs can do you a lot of damage. Some drugs are **legal** and others are **illegal**. All drugs are bad for you if used in the wrong way or if you take too much. This book will give you lots of information about different types of drugs. Then you can make up your own mind.

I didn't realize caffeine was a drug. I drink about three cups of coffee a day.

I've seen people using heroin on TV. It looks horrible – they inject it into their arm.

My Mum has a glass of wine nearly every night. That's okay though.

What should I do if someone offers me drugs?

Loads of my friends smoke, but I think it's disgusting!

illegal   against the law
legal   within the law

What is a drug?

A drug is a chemical substance that can affect your body and change your mood, the way you behave and how you feel. Drugs come in all shapes, forms and colours.

Alcohol

Alcohol is found in drinks like beer, lager, **alcopops**, cider, wine and spirits (see pages 12 to 13).

Tobacco

Tobacco contains a drug called **nicotine** (see pages 14 to 15).

Caffeine

Caffeine is found in coffee, tea, chocolate and some fizzy drinks (see page 19).

Illegal drugs

There are drugs that are against the law (like cannabis, cocaine, heroin, ecstasy, LSD). Many of these are very dangerous and harmful (see pages 20 to 31).

Steroids

Steroids can be used as medicines, but some body-builders and athletes use them to change their body shape (see page 18).

Medicines

Doctors **prescribe** medicines to make us feel better when we are unwell. We can also buy many medicines over the counter at the pharmacy (see pages 10 to 11).

Find out later...

Why do people take drugs?

Why is it important to make the right choice?

How do I get help?

nicotine   addictive, colourless liquid that is poisonous in large amounts
prescribe   to be given medicines by a doctor

5

Drugs around us

Teen quotes
People take drugs
for many reasons

Drugs are all around us. They are taken for different reasons.

Why do people take drugs?

The main reason that people take drugs is to change the way they are feeling. Feeling different does not always mean feeling better. The feelings that drugs give you do not last forever. Medicines are drugs and people take them to feel different or better. However, all drugs can be dangerous, some if used too much and some if used just once.

> I had period pain and my mum said that paracetamol would help.

> Loads of my friends were smoking, and I thought that it looked cool.

> Everyone was daring us to take the tablets, so we did, just for a laugh.

depressed   unhappy and gloomy
E   nickname for ecstasy tablet

People can take harmful drugs for a number of reasons. Here is one teenager's experience:

Ed's story

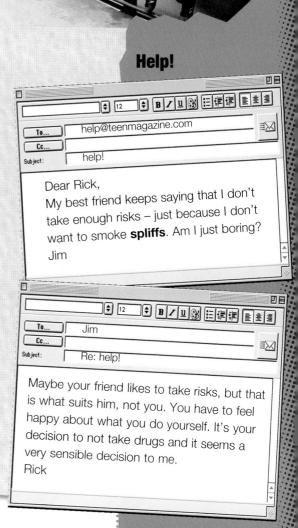

When I was fourteen I started to worry more about what people thought of me. My friends were taking **Es** sometimes, and I thought that it might make me feel more confident. So I tried one and it made me feel great at first. I wanted to take one every weekend so that I could go to parties and not feel so shy. Then I realized that I was feeling really low. A friend told me that this is what happens when the chemicals in the E leave your body. I decided it just was not worth it – taking something dangerous that was really making me more **depressed** in the end.

Help!

To... help@teenmagazine.com
Cc...
Subject: help!

Dear Rick,
My best friend keeps saying that I don't take enough risks – just because I don't want to smoke **spliffs**. Am I just boring?
Jim

To... Jim
Cc...
Subject: Re: help!

Maybe your friend likes to take risks, but that is what suits him, not you. You have to feel happy about what you do yourself. It's your decision to not take drugs and it seems a very sensible decision to me.
Rick

paracetamol   type of painkiller
spliff   rolled up cannabis cigarette

Why are some drugs alright, and others not?

Some people think it is strange that certain drugs that harm us are not against the law. **Nicotine**, in tobacco, and alcohol are seen as acceptable for people to take. This is because they are **legal**, but both drugs can damage your health. Other drugs like cannabis or cocaine are often seen as really bad because they are **illegal**. Read the views of these two teenagers and see what you think.

► ► ► ► ►
Find out all about cannabis on pages 22 and 23.

TRUE OR FALSE?

'Nicotine is one of the most addictive drugs used by humans.'

TRUE

Lots of people smoke cigarettes. They are not breaking the law and it is seen as being okay, even though it is not good for you. Nicotine in tobacco is one of the most addictive drugs that humans use, though.

I think that cannabis should be made legal and alcohol should be **banned**. Alcohol is so much more harmful for you.

No way. Alcohol is fine. Everyone drinks it and it just helps people relax. Cannabis is really bad for you.

addictive   makes the user dependent on a substance

Cannabis can help people who are in pain.

Okay, people who are sick might be able to use it, but it shouldn't be legal for everyone. It's too **addictive** and it might make people use **hard drugs**.

I don't need alcohol to enjoy myself.

Alcohol is a hard drug. It causes all sorts of health problems and some people get really violent when they are drunk.

I suppose so, but I think alcohol is fine with a meal or your family.

Did you know?

In some countries in the world, alcohol is illegal and therefore it is not seen as a good thing. Countries where lots of **Muslims** live, such as Pakistan, do not allow people to drink alcohol. They believe it is a powerful drug that affects the mind in a bad way.

Yeah, but what about when people drink and drive? Alcohol can kill the people who drink it and others around them. It's very addictive too, like a **poison** that some people can't do without.

hard drug drug that is particularly addictive or dangerous, like cocaine

Drugs in everyday life

My medicine

❝ I have **asthma** and have to use an **asthma inhaler**. I know that I should only use it like my doctor has told me. I also shouldn't let my friends use it, because it is quite a strong medicine. ❞

Lizzy, 13

The most obvious drugs that we see in everyday life are medicines.

Medicines

Medicines are drugs that can change the way you feel. For example, people take **paracetamol** to get rid of pain. Medicines come in different forms and are taken in different ways. They can be tablets or liquids, and can be swallowed, inhaled or injected. Medicines are only good if they have been **prescribed** for you by a doctor or given to you by a responsible adult.

Other people's medicines can be very dangerous for you. Medicines can also be very dangerous if taken in large amounts, or if you take different ones at the same time.

Labels

Read the labels on medicine packets and bottles and study the information leaflet carefully.

Zara's experience

Fifteen-year-old Zara had a terrible headache. She did not have any headache tablets, but she thought it would be alright if she took some of her Dad's backache pills. She found them in the medicine cupboard at home. She thought they must all be the same sort of medicine. She only took two of the pills, but they made her really sick. They were too strong for her and reacted badly in her stomach. Luckily she was okay, but if she had taken any more she could have ended up in hospital. Her Dad was very worried, but he is sure that Zara will never take anybody else's medicines again.

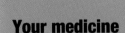

Your medicine

❝ Medicines have been tested so they are safe if they are used properly. It is very important to follow the instructions carefully and only take them if they are meant for you. ❞

Pharmacist

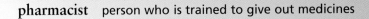

pharmacist   person who is trained to give out medicines

Alcohol

Why do people drink?

Sometimes I drink at parties to be **sociable**.

I drank alcohol once and it made me really sick.

My parents let me have a drink on birthdays and at weddings.

To... Lucy
Cc...
Subject: Alcopops

Last night we went out in town. We bought some **alcopops** from the supermarket – they tasted just like lemonade. It felt really cool to buy the drink when we're not yet eighteen. I had three bottles, and felt great for a while. It made me really chatty and I felt confident. Then suddenly I felt sick and dizzy and couldn't stand up! I can't remember what happened after that. Mum had to come and pick me up I was so ill. I was sick on the stairs at home and I'm not allowed out for the rest of the month. I won't drink that stuff again in a hurry. It made me feel awful.

Yasmin xx

◄ Alcohol can be hard to avoid at weddings.

blood pressure   pressure of the blood going around the body; a high blood pressure is dangerous

Body damage

Alcohol can seriously damage parts of your body if misused:

Brain
Alcohol damages your brain cells.

Heart
Your heart muscles will get weaker and your **blood pressure** will get higher. Your heart will have a lot of pressure on it, as it will have to work much harder.

Stomach
Alcohol eats away at your stomach lining causing stomach pain, **indigestion**, vomiting, diarrhoea and stomach **ulcers**.

Liver
Your liver will stop getting rid of the waste in your body. Your stomach will swell and your skin will get yellow and itchy.

What is a unit?
One unit is equal to one small glass of wine, or measure of spirits like gin or vodka, or around 250ml (half a pint) of standard strength beer, lager or cider.

What is safe?

Men = no more than 21 units per week, or 3 to 4 units per day.
Women = no more than 14 units per week, or 2 to 3 units per day.

It is **illegal** for anyone under the age of eighteen to buy alcohol in a pub or shop. This is because alcohol can damage your body as you are growing.

---

indigestion   difficulty digesting (breaking down) food in your stomach   13

Tobacco

Tobacco in cigarettes is full of the drug **nicotine**. This is a very powerful drug that affects the brain very quickly. It is also highly **addictive**. If tobacco is smoked for a long time it speeds up the heart rate. The cigarette smoke, which passes into the lungs, leaves behind a sticky brown **tar**. This tar contains chemicals that can cause cancer. When someone smokes, the body produces **mucus** to protect itself from the effects of tar. This can clog the air passages and lungs and stop them from working properly. Also, the heart has to work harder to get enough oxygen around the body. This can lead to heart attacks.

▼ This tobacco farm is on the island of Cuba.

▼ Look at these lungs. The lung on the left is from a non-smoker. The lung on the right has been badly damaged through smoking.

mucus   sticky fluid that can come out of your mouth and nose

Ask the doctor

Q How does smoking affect your body?

A When people smoke cigarettes they breathe chemicals straight into their lungs. This can cause coughs and chest problems. As well as damaging your lungs, smoking can also lead to cancer of the mouth and throat.

> **Gary:** Everyone is doing it. Come on Tayo, let's try a cigarette.
>
> **Tayo:** You must be joking. Everyone must be mad if they are doing it – it makes your breath stink!
>
> **Gary:** But it makes you look so cool.
>
> **Tayo:** What's cool about getting black lungs?

Damage

It is not just your health that suffers from cigarettes. Because so many people smoke around the world, growing tobacco makes lots of money. In places like Brazil, whole forests are being destroyed, so that even more tobacco plants can be grown. This means that there is not enough land for farming food. Also, it means that animals are losing their homes.

tar   brown, treacle-like substance that contains poisons

Solvents

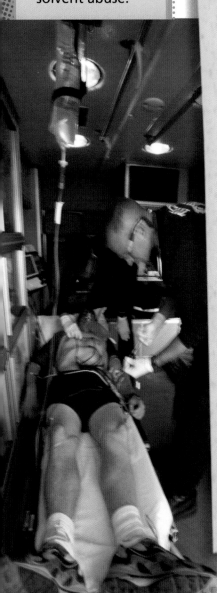

Did you know?

In Britain, about 75 young people die each year from solvent abuse.

Name of drug?
Solvents include gases, glue, aerosols (like hairspray), deodorant, paints, correcting fluid.

Nicknames?
Nose-bag, Stick-up, Spray.

What does it look like?
A substance found in glue, aerosols, lighter fluids, petrol and nail varnish remover.

What are the ups?
It might make you feel light-headed and see things that are not there.

What are the downs?
- It can make you feel sick, tired, and frightened.

- You might become **unconscious** and choke on your own vomit.

What is the damage?
- It can make you feel tired, **depressed** and unable to concentrate.

- It can cause brain damage, liver and kidney problems and even heart failure.

- Solvent abuse can be **fatal**, even for first time users.

fatal   result in death
suffocation   when someone is unable to breathe

Peter's story

I've always thought I was very safe. I'd never take risks. I suppose I'm usually too scared. I never used to nick sweets when other kids did. I'd never answer back to teachers and I never missed school. People thought I was a teacher's pet. Then one day, a friend wanted me to try sniffing glue. I knew it was dangerous, but they were all doing it and I felt left out. I tried it. What a mistake! I collapsed, was sick and was rushed to hospital. The doctor said I was lucky to be alive. I won't take risks like that again.

Doctor's warning

' Sniffing solvents can cause heart failure and **suffocation**. Heavy solvent abuse can lead to brain damage and kidney and liver failure. If you know anyone who sniffs solvents, help them to stop now. '

unconscious   passed out

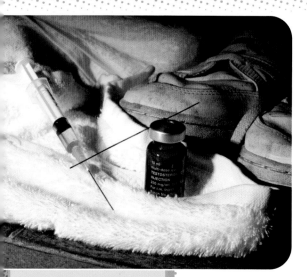

Misuse of drugs in sport

Steroids are used in medicine and there are lots of different types. You can get them on prescription from a doctor. For example, corticosteroids are used in **asthma inhalers**. Athletes sometimes use **anabolic steroids**. This is against the law, although there is a debate about whether this is fair or not.

Did you know?
Steroids can cause:

* very heavy acne on the face and back

* an increase in the size of boy's and men's breasts

* problems with **menstruation** in girls and women

* anxiety and panic attacks

* high **blood pressure** and **heart disease**.

Sammy's steroids

The crowd thought Sammy looked fantastic. He had been training for weeks and was the favourite to win the 400 metres race. But it all ended in tears for Sammy. He did win, by a long way. But when Sammy was tested for drugs, the test showed that he had been taking steroids to improve his performance. He was disqualified from the race. Sammy said, 'I just didn't want to let my team down by losing, but I have let them down now anyway. I feel like a cheat. I won't take the steroids any more and will win the race next year naturally.'

anabolic steroids   drugs that build body tissue
menstruation   another word for a girl's period

Caffeine

Caffeine is a **stimulant**. It makes the heart beat faster and wakes up the brain. It can be **addictive** if taken in large amounts. Lots of people around the world use caffeine to give them a boost of energy when they are feeling tired. It is a completely **legal** drug and is found in foods and drinks such as tea, coffee, cola, chocolate and energy drinks. However, like all drugs it is not good to take too much caffeine. If your body gets used to a lot of caffeine you will get really bad headaches when you do not eat or drink any.

How much?

How much caffeine do you drink in one day?

07:45

I am feeling sleepy, I had better have some coffee before school.

15:00

I need cola to wake me up for the English lesson.

19:00

I need an energy drink before I go out.

stimulant makes you feel awake and gives you lots of energy

Illegal drugs

Some drugs are **legal** and others are **illegal**. Drugs which people use illegally are very harmful. Some illegal drugs make people feel happy and excited, others make people feel relaxed, sleepy and dizzy. Some can make people have **hallucinations**. Many people who use illegal drugs start to need more and more of them. Find out more about illegal drugs on the following pages.

Heroin
(see pages 26 to 27)

Cannabis
(see pages 22 to 23)

Cocaine
(see pages 24 to 25)

hallucination   seeing or hearing something which is not there

Breaking the law

You do not just risk your health when you get involved with illegal drugs. You are also breaking the law and risk getting a criminal record. This can affect the rest of your life.

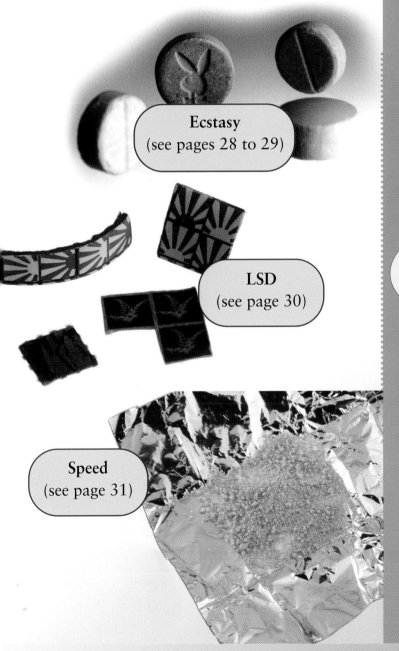

Ecstasy
(see pages 28 to 29)

LSD
(see page 30)

Speed
(see page 31)

Want to know more?

Find out the answers to these questions on the next few pages.

I want to know more about which drugs are illegal.

I've heard that drugs make you want to dance all night. Is this true?

What do drugs do to you?

21

Cannabis

TRUE OR FALSE?

'Smoking cannabis is not as harmful as smoking cigarettes.'

FALSE

People usually roll up joints using cannabis with tobacco, so you get the harmful effects of both drugs. Smoking anything is harmful.

Name of drug?
Cannabis

Nicknames?
Weed, grass, puff, gear, smoke, hash, ganja, draw.

What does it look like?
Cannabis comes as a hard, brown lump, or as a leaf with seeds and stalks, or as a dark oil.

What are the ups?
- Most people who smoke cannabis feel relaxed and talkative.
- They can feel like they are enjoying music and other things around them more.

What are the downs?
- Cannabis can make you feel very nervous and even **paranoid**.
- It can make you feel confused or dazed.
- Some people feel very hungry when they have smoked cannabis.

What is the damage?
- Because cannabis is usually smoked with tobacco, it is as bad for the body as smoking cigarettes.
- Cannabis affects the memory and the ability to concentrate.

Jasmine's diary

I was really excited about smoking a **joint** for the first time. I thought that it would make me feel relaxed and giggly – other people had said such great things about it.
But although it gave me the giggles for a while, it also made me feel nervous and strange, like I was paranoid. Then I felt dizzy and sick, so I don't think I will do it again.

What do you think?

People have different opinions about cannabis.

Cannabis is supposed to be really mild. I think it is less harmful than alcohol.

Because so many people use cannabis, some teenagers think it is **legal**, but it is not!

Once you start smoking cannabis, you might be tempted to try **hard drugs**.

paranoid   really worried and anxious. Feeling like everyone is looking at you or talking about you.

Cocaine

What would you do...

...if you were offered cocaine at a party?

I wouldn't do something that I didn't want to just because my friends were doing it.

I know it would be difficult, but I would walk away and try to talk to other people.

I would leave the party if I had to.

Name of drug?
Cocaine

Nicknames?
C, charlie, snow, coke, white.

What does it look like?
- Cocaine is a white powder that people snort up the nose.
- It can also be dissolved in water and injected.

What are the ups?
- Most people who snort cocaine will feel a buzz and feel good for about 30 minutes.
- They often feel energetic and more confident than usual.

What are the downs?
- As the effects stop, it can make you feel very **depressed** and fed up.
- Some people then take other drugs to make themselves feel better again.
- Because cocaine is **addictive**, people using it often crave more, which can become a very expensive habit.

What is the damage?
- Cocaine can cause heart problems and chest pains.
- Snorting cocaine can damage the inside of the nose.
- If you use cocaine a lot, you may feel confused and **paranoid**.
- If you inject with needles, you could pick up very dangerous, or even **fatal** infections.
- If you **overdose** on cocaine it can kill you.

crack   form of cocaine that you can smoke

Leon's story

Leon was looking forward to the party, but when he got there he realized that all his friends were snorting cocaine. He felt left out and was worried that they would laugh at him if he did not join in. So, he tried it himself. He remembers chatting a lot, but also feeling weird and paranoid. The next day and night he felt very lonely and tearful. He was really ill. When he realized this was another effect of the drug, he felt disappointed in himself.

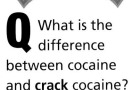

Q What is the difference between cocaine and **crack** cocaine?

A Crack is a form of cocaine that can be smoked. The effects are the same as for cocaine, but much stronger. The effects do not last as long as with cocaine. Crack is addictive, and people often crave more after taking it just once.

overdose taking too much of any drug

25

Q I found a syringe in my friend's coat pocket and I'm really worried that she has been injecting heroin. What should I do?

A This is serious. You need to help her immediately. Phone a drugs helpline and they will tell you where to get help.

Heroin

<u>Name of drug?</u>
Heroin

<u>Nicknames?</u>
Brown, gear, H, heaven, horse, junk, skag, smack.

<u>What does it look like?</u>
Light brown powder (or fluffy white when it is pure). It can be smoked, eaten, snorted or dissolved in water and injected.

<u>What are the ups?</u>
• It can make you feel relaxed.
• It might make your worries or pain feel like they are fading away.

<u>What are the downs?</u>
• It can make you sweaty and dizzy.
• It can affect your breathing and make you vomit and pass out.

<u>What is the damage?</u>
• It is very **addictive**.
• Heroin is often mixed with other substances, so you never really know what you are taking.
• If you inject it and use shared needles, you could catch very serious diseases such as **HIV**.
• It is easy to take an **overdose** and it can be **fatal**.

HIV disease that makes it difficult for the body to fight off infection

Jenny's story

Jenny had been going out with Steve for six months when she found out he took heroin. Steve wanted Jenny to try it, but she knew it was dangerous. Steve said she would try it if she loved him, so she let him inject her. At first it made them feel good together. But soon Jenny was addicted. One day she took too much and passed out. She nearly died. She went to a **re-hab centre** for help and it took over a year for her to get better. She is not with Steve now and is starting to get her life back together.

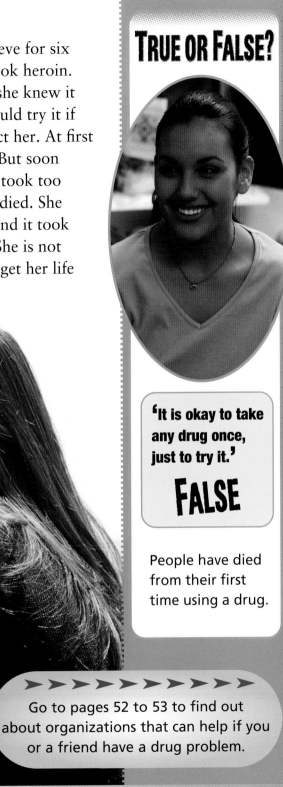

TRUE OR FALSE?

'It is okay to take any drug once, just to try it.'

FALSE

People have died from their first time using a drug.

▶ ▶ ▶ ▶ ▶ ▶ ▶ ▶ ▶ ▶ ▶

Go to pages 52 to 53 to find out about organizations that can help if you or a friend have a drug problem.

re-hab centre where people with drugs problems get help to live without drugs

Ecstasy

Name of drug?
Ecstasy

Nicknames?
E, fantasy, doves, dolphins, disco biscuits.

What does it look like?
- Small tablets or pills, usually white.
- Sometimes it is in a powder called MDMA.
- People usually swallow ecstasy tablets but sometimes they smoke or snort them.

What are the ups?
- Most people who take ecstasy feel very awake and full of energy.
- Takers may feel more aware of things around them, like sounds, colours and **emotions**.

What are the downs?
- As the chemicals in ecstasy start to work, some people feel their heartbeat increase, they sweat more and they might feel sick.
- After the effects of ecstasy have worn off, some people feel **depressed** for a few days.

What is the damage?
- Some of the effects of taking ecstasy are not known.
- Because ecstasy comes in the form of a tablet, you do not know exactly what you are taking and how it might affect you.
- People have died from the effects of ecstasy.

I am often offered ecstasy at parties, but I always say no.

I have taken an E once and I had a good time. But I was really scared about what could happen to me, so I won't do it again.

　emotions　feelings

Ecstasy girl dies on eighteenth birthday

Nicola Mbakwe died when she took an ecstasy tablet at her eighteenth birthday party. Police discovered that she and three of her close friends had bought ecstasy pills 'as a special treat'. According to her friends, it was the first time she had ever tried the drug.

Her parents were shocked and upset by the news, saying, 'It was such a stupid risk to take. She was so sensible and had her whole life ahead of her to have fun. We will never get over this awful loss.'

▲ Nicola Mbakwe had been preparing to go to college.

TRUE OR FALSE?

'Ecstasy will not do you any harm if you drink lots of water.'

FALSE

Drinking too much water in one go can be dangerous when you are taking ecstasy. It is better to sip a pint of water slowly every hour.

LSD

Name of drug?
LSD

Nicknames?
Acid, trips, blotters, dots.

What does it look like?
- Tiny squares of paper, often with a picture on one side.
- It causes an experience called a **trip** that can last up to twelve hours.

What are the ups?
- The effect depends on your mood at the time.
- If you are feeling good it will make you feel even better, but if you are feeling uncomfortable you will have a bad experience and feel confused, panicked and **depressed**.

What are the downs?
It can give you bad **hallucinations**, like your worst nightmares.

What is the damage?
- It can make you feel **paranoid** or out of control and can leave users shaken for a long time.
- Accidents may happen when hallucinating.
- It can cause mental problems such as depression and anxiety.
- You could have **flashbacks**.

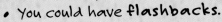

► LSD blotters seized at a party. This photo was taken in a police station.

flashback uncontrollable, dream-like moments that recall unpleasant events

◀ Students sometimes turn to speed if they are under a lot of pressure.

Speed

Q&A

Name of drug?
Speed
Nicknames?
Whizz, uppers, sulphate, amph.
What does it look like?
- Grey, white or dirty-white powder or tablets.
- It can be snorted, swallowed, injected or smoked.

What are the ups?
- It is a **stimulant**.
- It makes the heart beat faster and may give you lots of energy.
- Some people feel more confident when they have taken it.
- Some people use it to keep themselves awake so they can study more.

What are the downs?
- It can make you feel tired and depressed after you have taken it.

What is the damage?
- Your sleep and memory can be damaged.
- If you use it a lot it can make you paranoid and it puts a strain on the heart.

Q I went to a club the other night, and some of my friends were trying to get me to take speed. I said no, but what if they ask me again?

A You do not have to do anything you do not want to do. Be strong and tell them that you are not interested. If they still try to make you, think about whether they really are your friends or not.

trip   feeling like being in a dream (sometimes good and sometimes bad)

Drugs and the law

Young criminals

> **❝** I never thought it could happen to me. I didn't even want to try drugs. I didn't mean to end up a criminal either. Both of these things just happened. **❞**
>
> *Ellie, 16.*

It is not just drugs that are against the law. Many people break the law to get money to pay for drugs.

Drugs and crime

Drug users can end up stealing, even from friends and family. One thing leads to another and serious crimes are committed. It might just start by taking your mum's cigarettes but things can quickly get out of control. Nothing will stand in the way of people getting the drugs they need.

> **❝** I was really and truly sorry, but it didn't stop me from being sent to prison. **❞**
>
> *Chris, 16.*

Mark's story

Here is one drug addict's story:

'I started smoking when I was twelve. We used to drink a lot, too, and I remember stealing a bottle of vodka a few times. Then we started smoking cannabis and that was even more expensive. Before I knew it, I was trying cocaine, and then heroin. I was still at school and I needed cash to buy the drugs so I did some terrible things. I stole my Nan's credit card, I sold cannabis to kids at school and I broke into houses. I ended up in prison for two years. Now that I am out of prison, I've got to start over again. One thing I won't be doing is drugs.'

Did you know?
The police could charge you if they think that you have been getting drugs to sell or give to your friends. Your name will be kept on police records for five years. If you have a criminal record, you may not be able to go abroad or get your ideal job.

33

The law

Most drugs are **illegal**. If the police think you are carrying an illegal drug, they can make you turn out your pockets. They can also take you to the police station and search you. In the UK, if the police find drugs on you, they can charge you for two reasons:

- 'Possession': Being caught with an illegal drug for your own use. They will tell your parents or carer and sometimes social services. Your name will be kept on their records.

- 'Supplying drugs or possession with intent to supply drugs': This means that you had the drugs to give to someone else, even if it was your friend who asked you to get them. The punishment could be very severe.

What do you think?

I can't imagine having to go to prison.

I've got a criminal record. Now it's harder for me to get a job.

The police tell your parents if they find you with drugs.

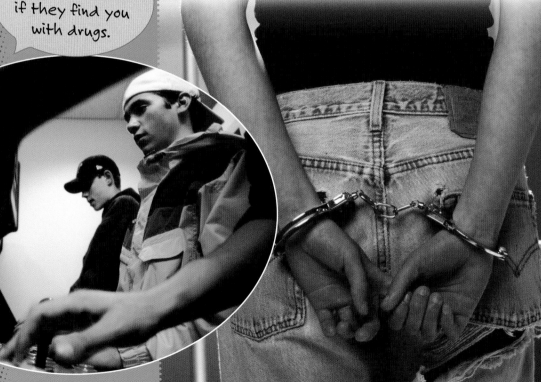

barbiturates   drug used to help people relax

Drug classes

Drugs in the UK are divided into three classes.

Class	Drugs	Possession	Supplying
A	Cocaine, ecstasy, heroin, LSD, speed prepared for injection	7 year prison sentence and/or a fine	Life imprisonment and/or a fine
B	Speed, **barbiturates**	5 year prison sentence and/or a fine	14 year prison sentence and/or a fine
C	Cannabis, most **anabolic steroids, tranquillizers** such as **Rohypnol**	2 year prison sentence and/or a fine	5 year prison sentence and/or a fine

In the state of Victoria, Australia, drug possession and supply is punished severely. The worst sentences are for Class A drugs, like heroin, and can be up to 25 years in prison for supplying. Class C drugs, like steroids, have a maximum penalty of two years in prison.

◀◀◀◀◀◀◀◀◀◀◀◀◀◀
Go to pages 12 to 15 to find out more about the effects of alcohol and tobacco.

Did you know?

- It is illegal to sell alcohol in shops and bars to people who are under eighteen.

- It is illegal to sell cigarettes to people who are under sixteen.

tranquillizers   drug used to make people feel calm

Drugs and other people

Q My brother is addicted to cocaine. What should I do?

A Your brother needs lots of support from you and your family and from health professionals too. Contact your local doctor and find a helpline.

When someone misuses a drug, it does not just affect that person's life. It affects the lives of all the people around them.

Families and relationships

Lucy was fifteen when she started drinking alcohol heavily with her friends. It had always been a laugh, but slowly Lucy began to feel nervous and shaky if she had not had alcohol that day. Sometimes, when she woke up she wanted to drink vodka just to feel normal and in control again. Her teachers noticed that her breath smelt and she was not turning up for class. They asked to see Lucy's parents who went mad and grounded her for two weeks. This just made things worse.

Lucy had massive arguments with her parents. She wanted to leave home and be on her own. Her parents also felt angry and let down. Finally, though, they got to see a good doctor who helped Lucy get control of her life back.

Lucy's friends were worried, too:

> ❝ She was so out of control, I didn't know how to help her. ❞

> ❝ She frightened me when she was drunk, because it was like she didn't care about anything. ❞

> ❝ My mum told me to stay away from Lucy when she realized Lucy had a drinking problem. I felt very bad, but what could I do? ❞

Drug stress

> ❝ Even though I loved my boyfriend, I loved cocaine more. When we were out, I kept thinking about it and wanting to be with other friends who were taking it. I hated my boyfriend telling me to stop, so we broke up. I really regret that now – we could still be together. ❞

Kamal's drug problems

'I knew that Kamal had changed. He seemed more distant and like he didn't care about stuff as much as he used to. I also knew that he was hanging out with a crowd of lads who sniff a lot of glue. I tried to talk to Kamal about it but he just got really annoyed with me and told me to mind my own business. If we hadn't been such good mates, I think I would have done that, but I really cared about what happened to him. So, I found some websites and helplines for people who use drugs and sent them to him.'

'You need special training to help someone who is addicted to drugs.'

TRUE

If someone is addicted to drugs, nurses and doctors who are specially trained can help them. The person addicted also needs lots of support from their family and friends.

‘ At first Kamal didn't respond, but he soon emailed me back and asked to meet. He was sure that his gang was getting into small crime like stealing and stuff and he really wasn't into that. So, after lots of talking he decided to contact the websites and got some advice on how to get out of trouble. It was such a relief, because I know how dangerous glue-sniffing is. Also, it means that we can be good friends again. ’

Justin, aged 14.

Websites and helplines have usually got lots of advice for people who are worried about their friends or family taking drugs.

Q What can I do if my friend refuses to accept help with his drug problem?

A Keep supporting him and making sure that he knows where to go for help when he is ready. Tell someone else about his problem, so that you don't have to cope with it on your own.

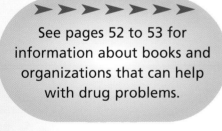

See pages 52 to 53 for information about books and organizations that can help with drug problems.

Giving up

Giving up drugs is tough. Lots of support is needed from professionals, friends and family.

Addiction

Addiction is when drug taking gets out of control, and you find it hard not to take the drug. The drug takes over – all your time, your energy and money are spent on getting hold of it. People get addicted to the feeling the drug gives, so they take it again and again. They need to take more to get the same feeling, and then more and more. This is called building up **tolerance** to a drug. Drug addiction does not happen overnight, but it does not take very long.

tolerance   the body's ability to cope with a drug

Jerome's story

One year ago, a friend made Jerome snort some cocaine. It gave him a nice feeling and he thought it would be okay to do it again. Within two weeks, he needed cocaine every day. It was expensive and he spent all his money on the drug. He became very ill and lost all his friends. Someone found him **unconscious** one day. They rushed him to hospital and managed to revive him. He now lives in a **re-hab centre** where he is being looked after. He admits he would never want to go through all that again. Jerome was lucky. Not everybody has a happy ending to their story.

Phone help

Hello, I'm worried that I am addicted to alcohol. I need to have a drink when I get in from school because I feel so stressed. What should I do?

Well, you've phoned the right place, we can help you. Let's talk about it.

41

Realizing that you need help

Lots of people take drugs for lots of different reasons. Sometimes, it is just a phase that teenagers will go through and then grow out of. However, it is also true that many young people have problems with drugs. It is important to know when you are taking too many risks with your health and when you need help.

Talk
Who would you talk to about drugs?

I would go to my teacher or my older sister.

If I couldn't go to family or friends, I would talk to my doctor.

I would find it very difficult to go to my parents, but I might turn to my aunt.

Answer the questions below to see if you might need help with drugs.

- Do you take drugs more than twice a week?
- Do you enjoy taking drugs much more than your friends?
- Do you get greedy when taking drugs?
- Do you crave the buzz of drugs all the time?
- Do you like to take drugs on your own?
- Are you worried about how many drugs you take?

If your answer to any of the questions opposite was 'Yes', you really need to talk to someone about your drug use. The first person you turn to might be a friend or someone in your family. Make sure that you talk to someone you can trust. How about talking to a doctor or nurse? Search on the Internet for websites that will give you advice.

Q I have started drinking alcohol a lot, even when I'm on my own. I feel nervous if I haven't had any for a couple of days. Have I got a problem?

A It does sound like you need alcohol quite a lot. It is very good that you are being so honest about it. Go and see your doctor and explain the problem. Also, talk to any other adult that you trust and ask them to help you.

How to get help

Who would you turn to?

- Friends
- Sister or brother
- Parents
- Teachers
- Doctor or nurse
- Problem page
- Phone helpline
- Websites

I had always been a bit nervous of phone helplines. I thought they were just for people that had no friends. Then I started taking LSD with some friends. It was a laugh at first but then I started feeling quite low and had some bad experiences on the drug. I also began to panic about things that were really stupid. I thought that it might be the drug but I felt silly asking anyone. My teacher had told us about this number, so I rang the helpline. When they first answered I almost put the phone down.

44

The person on the other end of the phone sounded quite young and really friendly. He asked if I wanted to talk about anything and said that he would not tell anyone. That was a real relief. He was so calm and had lots of time to listen to me, so I opened up and told him my worries. Just talking to someone made me feel so much better. I knew that he couldn't just make my problem go away, but I felt more able to deal with it. I came off the phone feeling much more in control. I am now sure that I want to give up LSD for good.

Doctor's opinion

' I will always see teenagers, even without their parents. I think it is important that they know there is someone they can talk to. I see lots of young people with a whole range of worries and problems. I just give them advice and some telephone numbers of other people who can help. '

Dr Singh

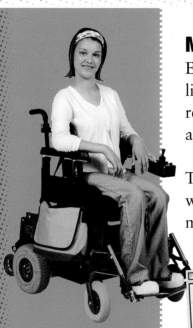

Making choices

Everyone has to make choices and decisions in life. As you get older you have to start taking responsibility for yourself. Sometimes decisions are easy and sometimes they are hard.

There are always people you can ask for advice, who are happy to help. But really you have to make up your own mind. The choice is yours.

Remember

- Be confident in yourself.

- Think about how your actions will affect you and other people.

- Speak to other people and ask for their advice.

- Think sensibly about all the options you have.

- Make sure you make the right decision for you.

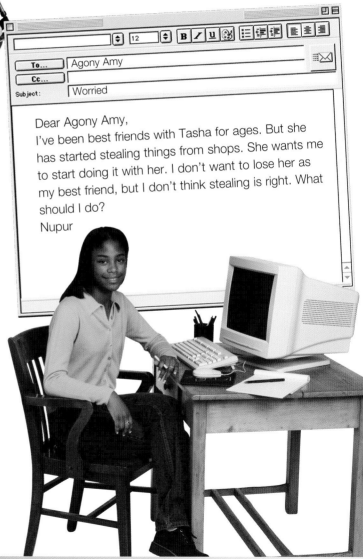

To... Agony Amy
Cc...
Subject: Worried

Dear Agony Amy,
I've been best friends with Tasha for ages. But she has started stealing things from shops. She wants me to start doing it with her. I don't want to lose her as my best friend, but I don't think stealing is right. What should I do?
Nupur

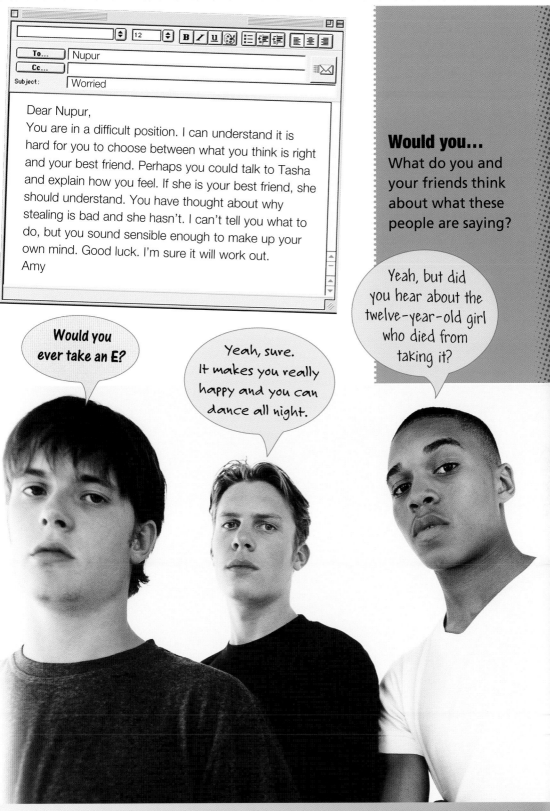

Dear Nupur,

You are in a difficult position. I can understand it is hard for you to choose between what you think is right and your best friend. Perhaps you could talk to Tasha and explain how you feel. If she is your best friend, she should understand. You have thought about why stealing is bad and she hasn't. I can't tell you what to do, but you sound sensible enough to make up your own mind. Good luck. I'm sure it will work out.

Amy

Would you...
What do you and your friends think about what these people are saying?

Yeah, but did you hear about the twelve-year-old girl who died from taking it?

Would you ever take an E?

Yeah, sure. It makes you really happy and you can dance all night.

All my friends are doing it

Sometimes people feel under pressure from their friends. Good friends would never make you do something you do not want to do. They should respect your decision. Sometimes people say they have done things because they think it makes them look cool. Often they are making it up.

What do you think?

Once I told my friend that I had started smoking. I hadn't really. I just thought it would impress her.

Sometimes it is hard to say no, especially when it's your friends.

I stick up for what I think is right.

Sophie's Diary

14th June

Dear Diary,

I can't believe Alicia and Tomi keep going on about how they are smoking **joints**. They think it is so cool. They even tried to make me do it. Chanise told me it's just as bad as smoking. I think Tomi will go off me if I don't do it soon, but I think they are stupid, so I don't care!

Agony Aunt

Dear Viv,
I feel really bad because I lied to my best
*friend. I told him I had taken an **E** at the*
weekend, but I hadn't. I just wanted to
impress my mates. What should I do? Please
help me.
Femi.

Dear Femi,
I think you know what you should do.
You're feeling bad about lying, and it
could harm your friendship. Why not tell
your friend the truth and put it all behind
you? I'm sure your mates like you for who
you are.
Good luck.
Viv

TRUE OR FALSE?

'You should
always stick up
for your friends.'

FALSE

Your friends are
not always right
and do not always
tell the truth.
Stick up for what
you believe in.

Your life, your choice

Not for me

There are some people at school who take drugs. I keep out of their way, because there is no way I want to get in to it.

This book has told you about lots of different drugs and things related to drugs. Do not forget that making good decisions means having lots of information. Also, you need to think carefully about what will happen to you, your family and your friends if you make an unwise choice.
In this book, you have heard the views of lots of young people. They all have different opinions and experiences of drugs. Now that you have all of this information you can make up your own mind about what you do. You are responsible for yourself.

I know lots about drugs and I think they are dangerous.

Talk helps

Remember, it is always good to talk about things like drugs. You can find out what your friends and family think. Also, you can discuss who you would turn to if you had a problem. Most people will understand and will want to help you. So do not worry about things on your own. Share your thoughts with others.

My friend thinks she looks cool smoking. I think she looks pathetic. I never want to smoke, it's disgusting!

I think drinking alcohol is alright for adults, but not too often and not too much.

One of my Dad's friends died of a heroin overdose.

Find out more

Organizations in the UK

Adfam
Adfam provides confidential support and information to anyone who is worried about a friend, or someone in the family, who is using drugs.
www.adfam.org.uk

Ash
Information for people concerned about cigarette smoking, whether they are smokers or spend time with smokers.
www.ash.org

Lifebytes
A fun and informative website that gives young people information to help them make their own choices about life.
www.lifebytes.gov.uk

Books

Get Real: Coping with friends, Kate Tym and Penny Worms (Raintree, 2004)

Need to know: Cocaine, Sean Connolly (Heinemann Library, 2003)

Need to know: Ecstasy, Sean Connolly (Heinemann Library, 2002)

What's at Issue? Drugs and You, Bridget Lawless (Heinemann Library, 2000)

Organizations in Australia

The Alcohol and other Drug Council of Australia
This website gives an overview of drug awareness organizations in Australia. Most of their work is carried out over the Internet.
www.adca.org.au

Australia Drug Foundation
The Australian Drug Foundation has a wide range of information on all aspects of drugs, their effects and their legal position in Australia.
www.adf.org.au

Centre for Education and Information on Drugs and Alcohol
A great contact for information on drug programmes across Australia. It also has one of the most extensive libraries on drug-related subjects in the world.
www.ceida.net.au

Organizations in the UK

National Drugs Helpline
Tel: 0800 77 66 00
This helpline provides a free telephone contact for all aspects of drug use and has a database covering all of the UK for further information about specific drugs or regional information.
www.ndh.org.uk

Quit
A national charity that helps people give up smoking.
www.quit.org.uk

Release
A website that looks at the health, welfare and legal needs of drug users. It includes an overview of different drugs and an analysis of the effects of each.
www.release.org. uk

Glossary

addictive makes the user dependent on a substance

alcopops strong, sweet tasting alcoholic drinks

anabolic steroids drugs that build body tissue, often used in sport

asthma condition that makes breathing difficult

asthma inhaler device for giving medicine to people with asthma

banned stopped

barbiturate drug used to help people relax

blood pressure pressure of the blood going around the body; a high blood pressure is dangerous

crack form of cocaine that you can smoke

depressed unhappy and gloomy

E nickname for ecstasy tablet

emotions feelings

fatal result in death

flashback uncontrollable, dream-like moments that recall unpleasant events

hallucination seeing or hearing something which is not there

hard drug drug that is particularly addictive or dangerous, like cocaine

heart disease damage to the heart which stops it working properly

HIV disease that makes it difficult for the body to fight off infection

illegal against the law

indigestion difficulty digesting (breaking down) food in your stomach

joint rolled up cannabis cigarette

legal within the law

MDMA scientific name for ecstasy

menstruation another word for a girl's period

mucus sticky fluid that can come out of your mouth and nose

Muslim someone who follows the religion of Islam

nicotine addictive, colourless liquid that is poisonous in large amounts

overdose taking too much of any drug

paracetamol type of painkiller

paranoid really worried and anxious. Feeling like everyone is looking at you or talking about you.

pharmacist person who is trained to give out medicines

poison very harmful substance

prescribe to be given medicines by a doctor

re-hab centre where people with drugs problems get help to live without drugs

Rohypnol date-rape drug which is also a tranquillizer

sociable like being around other people

spliff rolled up cannabis cigarette

stimulant makes you feel awake and gives you lots of energy

suffocation when someone is unable to breathe

tar brown, treacle-like substance that contains poisons

tolerance the body's ability to cope with a drug

tranquillizers drug used to make people feel calm

trip feeling like being in a dream (sometimes good and sometimes bad)

ulcer painful sore that heals very slowly

unconscious passed out

Index